Looking After Me

Taking Medicine

Crabtree Publishing Company

www.crabtreebooks.com

Crabtree Publishing Company

www.crabtreebooks.com   1-800-387-7650

Copyright © **2009 CRABTREE PUBLISHING COMPANY.**
All rights reserved. No part of this publication may be reproduced,
stored in a retrieval system or be transmitted in any form or by any
means, electronic, mechanical, photocopying, recording, or otherwise,
without the prior written permission of Crabtree Publishing Company.

Published in Canada
Crabtree Publishing
616 Welland Ave.
St. Catharines, ON
L2M 5V6

Published in the United States
Crabtree Publishing
PMB16A
350 Fifth Ave., Suite 3308
New York, NY 10118

Senior editor
Jennifer Schofield

Proofreader
Crystal Sikkens

Designer
Sophie Pelham

Project coordinator
Robert Walker

Digital color
Carl Gordon

Production coordinator
Margaret Amy Salter

Editor
Molly Aloian

Prepress technician
Katherine Kantor

Copy editor
Adrianna Morganelli

First published in 2008 by Wayland
338 Euston Road
London NW1 3BH

Wayland Australia
Level 17/207 Kent Street
Sydney NSW 2000

Copyright © Wayland 2008

Wayland is a division of
Hachette Children's Books,
a Hachette Livre UK company.

Library and Archives Canada Cataloguing in Publication

Gogerly, Liz
     Taking medicine / Liz Gogerly ; illustrator, Mike Gordon.

(Looking after me)
Includes index.
ISBN 978-0-7787-4114-5 (bound).--ISBN 978-0-7787-4121-3 (pbk.)

     1. Drugs--Juvenile fiction. 2. Drugs--Safety measures--
Handbooks, manuals, etc. I. Gordon, Mike II. Title. III. Series:
Gogerly, Liz. Looking after me.

PZ7.G562Ta 2008   j823'.92   C2008-903644-1

Library of Congress Cataloging-in-Publication Data

Gogerly, Liz.
     Taking medicine / written by Liz Gogerly ;
illustrated by Mike Gordon.
          p. cm. -- (Looking after me)
     Includes index.
     ISBN-13: 978-0-7787-4121-3 (pbk. : alk. paper)
     ISBN-10: 0-7787-4121-4 (pbk. : alk. paper)
     ISBN-13: 978-0-7787-4114-5 (reinforced library binding : alk. paper)
     ISBN-10: 0-7787-4114-1 (reinforced library binding : alk. paper)
     1. Drugs--Juvenile literature. I. Gordon, Mike. II. Title. III. Series.

RM301.17.G64 2009
615--dc22
                                                    2008025363

Looking After Me

Taking Medicine

Written by Liz Gogerly
Illustrated by Mike Gordon

I used to think
medicine was
like magic.

A spoonful of syrup made a cough disappear.

Taaadaaa!!

A little bit of cream made an itchy rash vanish.

A syringe of special pink liquid stopped a high temperature.

One day, I thought
I'd try my magic out
on my old teddy, Jack.

I pretended I was a doctor
and he was my patient.

Luckily for Jack there was a bottle of medicine on the counter. I was going to save his life!

But, still Jack
didn't look right.

So, I searched everywhere for more magic medicine.

I discovered some pills next to Mom's bed, and gave Jack five.

9

That's when Mom found us...
She was very angry!

She explained that I should never EVER play with medicines.

"Jimmy, pills aren't candy!"

I thought that medicines
always made you better.

But they can make you sick if you take the wrong amount.

Sometimes you should take your medicine after eating and other times you can't eat anything at all.

Mom made some new rules about medicines. All pills, special mixtures, and creams were locked away.

Soon after the new rules, my dad had a cough and a sore throat.

Mom gave him some cough syrup and throat lozenges.

The lozenge soothed his throat
and soon he stopped coughing.

I caught Dad's cough. Mom gave me some cough syrup and made me a hot drink with lemon and honey.

But, I still had a temperature
and a terrible earache so
Mom took me to the doctor.

He said I had an ear infection and I needed antibiotics to make me better.

We took the prescription
to the pharmacy.

I needed three
spoons of the
medicine before
food, three
times a day.

Mom put the medicine high
up where I couldn't reach it.

After a few days my earache was gone!

Even though I felt better, it was important to finish all the antibiotics.

I know now that medicine is not really magic and there are different kinds of medicine, too.

My grandfather has pills for his heart.

Jemima and Sally use inhalers because they have asthma.

Sometimes we get injections to protect us from illness or disease.

Special creams can help soothe a bee sting.

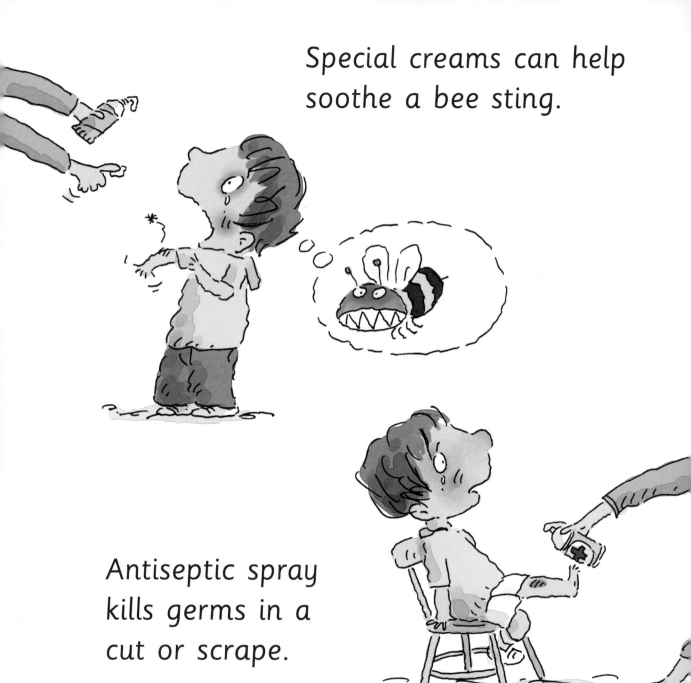

Antiseptic spray kills germs in a cut or scrape.

Mom says you don't always
need medicine to get better.
Sometimes a good rest will
do the trick.

Eating healthy food and getting a lot of exercise will keep you fit and strong.

NOTES FOR PARENTS AND TEACHERS

SUGGESTIONS FOR READING
LOOKING AFTER ME: TAKING MEDICINES
WITH CHILDREN

In this book, we meet Jimmy, a young boy who learns that there's more to medicine than magic. At the start of the story, he's playing with his teddy and manages to find some medicine. This would be a good time to talk to the children about what they think medicine does. Children often think that medicine will always make you better. The message of this book is that medicine can also be dangerous. Whether the medicine is an over-the-counter drug or a prescription, it could still be a danger.

In the next section of the book, Jimmy's parents introduce some house rules about medicine – simple rules that all caregivers should follow. Children will all have their own stories about where and how medicine is stored in their houses. It is important to stress that children should never tamper with bottles and try to open them. If they see pills in cardboard packages, they should leave them alone.

Some children may not understand the difference between prescription and non-prescription medicines. When Jimmy's father is sick he uses over-the-counter drugs. However, when Jimmy is sick he needs stronger medicine that can fight his ear infection. Jimmy's experience introduces children to how we get prescription medicines. Children may already know this process and you can encourage them to talk about their own experiences. The story also aims to show that some medicines are necessary for saving people's lives.

Jimmy's grandfather needs medication for his heart and his friends need inhalers for their asthma. Perhaps the children can think of other drugs or medicines that people take to save their lives. The book ends on a high note. Medicines are there to help us, and, if they are used correctly, they usually do make us better. However, our bodies are also amazing healing machines and as well as taking medicine, we can help keep ourselves healthy by eating well and keeping fit.

LOOKING AFTER ME AND CURRICULUM EXPECTATIONS

The Looking After Me series is designed to teach young readers the importance of personal hygiene, proper nutrition, exercise, and personal safety. This series supports key K-4 health education standards in Canada and the United States, including those outlined by the American Association for Health Education. According to these standards, students will

- Describe relationships between personal health behaviors and individual well being
- Explain how childhood injuries and illnesses can be prevented or treated
- Identify responsible health behaviors
- Identify personal health needs
- Demonstrate strategies to improve or maintain personal health
- Demonstrate ways to avoid and reduce threatening situations

BOOKS TO READ

First Look At: Do I have to go to hospital
Pat Thomas (Wayland 2008)
Helping Hands: In the doctor's surgery
Ruth Thomson (Wayland 2006)
The Big Day: Going to Hospital
Nicola Barber (Wayland 2008)

ACTIVITY:

Present children with a selection of packaging for medicines and ask them to decide how they know that they are not packaging for food or candy. Then, together with the children, make a collage or display to illustrate packaging for medicines and how they help medicines to be used safely. Talk with children about the use of medicines and when we may need them.

INDEX

32

Printed in China